An Ode
The Craft Gin

By David Hitchens

Gins of Heaven

Had I the heavens' embroidered gins,
Enwrought with juniper and citrus bright,
The coriander, cardamom and the dark gins
Of herb and spice giving the hearts cut,
I would spread out the gins in your sight:
But I, can only pour, that which I dream;
A liquid, my dream, so pure in your sight
Sip softly, because you sip of my dream.

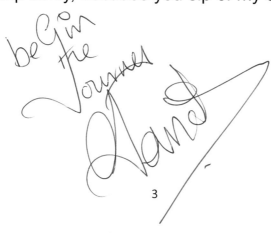

3

Index

Chapter 1

Gin: What is it and what does it taste like?

Why has Gin become so popular?

How are the different styles of gin made?

Chapter 2

Making sense of a 1000 Gins

How to taste Gin

Gin styles and reading the Gin map

Beverage Analysis Reference (B.A.R.) system

Chapter 3

Making sense of Gin styles

Other Gin styles

Chapter 4

Making sense of tonics

What is Tonic and why is it so important?

Tonic styles and the Gin map

The Gin - Tonic Scales

Chapter 5

Making sense of Garnishes

What is this book about?

Currently there are over a 1000 different Gins available to try and sample. Each may require one of at least seven different styles of tonics and/or garnishes to ensure the perfect G &T.

If you tried a new Gin every week it would take you over 19 years to sample every combination. So how do you make sense of a 1000 Gins? Just like a pile of jigsaw pieces - where do you start, what do you try next?

Ideally, you need to know at a glance what the possible combinations are, just like the lid on a jigsaw box shows how all the pieces fit together.

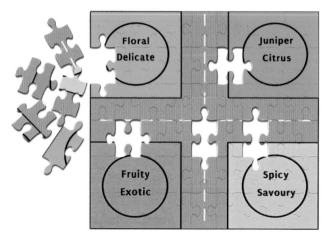

Then you need a road map, or ideally a Sat Nav, that shows where you are and the route you can take to get where you want to go.

This book introduces you to the 'Gin Sat Nav' that ultimately will help you identify your Gin Preference Style.

So…..Why is this the best approach? Read on and see how the world of Gin has changed in recent times.

Chapter 1

Gin: What is it and what does it taste like?

Essentially, Gin is juniper flavoured vodka that tastes like Christmas trees! ...... the juniper berry is the female seed cone from the juniper conifer tree, but the complexity of the elements found in this 'berry' add far more than just a pine like taste. It will offer hints of leather, fruit, citrus, grassy peppery and some sweet notes, all of which depends on where the berries have been grown.

Historically the juniper berry has been used for medicinal purposes, first recorded as being used by the Sumerians some 4000 years ago and still being used this way right through to the present day.

Often the technique to administer this as a medicine was to grind the berries down into a powder then mix with some form of alcohol to form a linctus.

By the 16th century the art of distilling improved dramatically and the 'Gin' was born as a social lubricant. The proponents of Science and Medicine met and were able to declare Gin was good for you!

Why has Gin become so popular?

Gin is versatile, you can have it short, have it long, have it strong or have it weak… with champagne or with tonic… with garnish or botanicals. The combinations are almost endless but most importantly they are fun and all taste good.

Most people have grown up with Gordon's as **the** Gin and tonic (with a slice of lemon of course!), which could be seen in a bar just about anywhere.

About a decade ago Hendrick's broke the mould by producing a Gin that allowed a flavour, other than the classic "dry juniper with a slight citrus twist", to come to the fore by using cucumber. Adding a slice of fresh cucumber rather than lemon to the drink made a new perfect serve.

Meanwhile Bombay Sapphire were redefining how Gin could be produced, by suspending their botanicals so that only the fumes of the alcohol went through them before extracting the essential oils. This resulted in a premium, much lighter, elegant and delicate floral type of Gin.

The Hendrick's approach sparked off a revolution which has resulted in many fruit dominant flavoured Gins and the Bombay sapphire approach has resulting in many complex and elegant Gins.

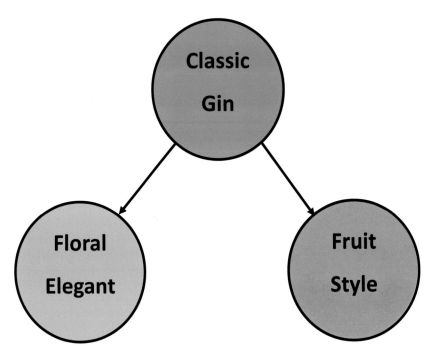

These two new styles broke the glass ceiling on what a Gin should be. This allowed manufacturers artistic license to experiment and see what further flavours and styles could be created.

Modern technology has made Gin making easier, and now the range is only limited by the imagination of the manufacturer as to what botanicals work well together.

Today there are over a thousand Gins available, all with their unique points of difference. What makes Gin particularly special as a drinking category is that the very nature of how it is made, allows a sophistication in flavours that can readily be identified and appreciated.

The elements of the flavour are purified by distillation, so that when the particle of the flavour touches your taste buds the clarity and distinctiveness of that flavour is identifiable.

The volume of the drink does not affect the quality of the flavours in the finished drink. This cannot be said for liqueurs or cordials, which is why gin acts as an ideal base to so many wonderful cocktails.

Traditionally, a mixologist in cocktail bars made the tonics live on site, using syrups and bitters according to the finish required. Fever Tree (a major tonic supplier) have created several standard styles of tonics using natural ingredients. Now, we the general public, can grab a gin and the appropriate tonic, pour the two together and achieve 75% of what a mixologist would have done.

Knowing what garnishes to use to get the perfect combination has been made easier with the use of phone apps for Gin. Now we ordinary folk can produce a drink that is almost as perfect as a mixologist would have made for us.

It is this 'I can do' thing that is happening that makes it fun. If we get it slightly wrong, who cares! as long as it still tastes good.

How are the different styles of Gin made?

Armed with a knowledge of the science of distilling and an understanding of the elements in each botanical (i.e. any part of a plant) over a 1000 different flavour profiles for Gin are now being produced.

Having decided on a mix of botanicals, the Gin maker uses one of the following methods to make the Gin.

A) Soak the botanicals in a clear spirit and let the flavours be extracted by the alcohol. Then filter the 'bits' out, then bottle (compound method). Most liqueurs are made this way.

B) Soak as before but then distill the spirit (boil the alcohol and botanical mix in a confined space) and let the vapours condense into a tank, ready for bottling. This method gives very distinctive flavours.

C) Put all the botanicals into a metal 'tea bag' and suspend this over the boiling alcohol. The fumes work their way through the tea bag extracting the required elements and then condensing into a tank ready for bottling. This method gives a much lighter, more delicate flavour finish.

D) Do all of C above, then add, for example, when making a raspberry gin, fresh raspberries, and let the finished Gin take on the colour and fresh taste of raspberries. Then filter to remove all the 'bits of raspberries', then bottle.

Chapter 2

Making sense of a 1000 Gins

How do you classify and make sense of the vast array of Gins available? How do you log them in a meaningful way that is not onerous on the brain and the liver?

Firstly, you need to establish what your own Gin preference is and in a format that can be easily understood. The jigsaw approach is an easy way to get a quick overview.

Then, for a Gin that you have tasted and liked, you need to find the position on the jigsaw for that Gin.

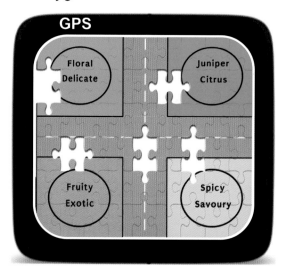

Gin Preference Style (the "GPS")

From there, if you want to taste different styles of Gin you can navigate your way round the jigsaw, just like using a "Sat Nav", and then fine tune your preferences.

First you need to know how to taste Gin correctly.....

How to taste Gin

Accurately assessing styles and allocating to the correct spot on the map, requires a consistent approach to the Gin tasting process.

Once you have experimented with a few gins and are confident about what to look for then you will find it easy to allocate a GPS reference for any Gin you try.

Palate

Start with a clean palate. Professional tasters cleanse their palate **by sniffing fresh coffee beans!**
Make sure the Gin is at room temperature and don't use ice at this stage.

Look

Take a look at your Gin in the glass. The majority of gins are clear but some botanicals can affect the colour.

Sniff

Swirl the Gin in the glass to release the aromas. Then with your nose a few inches from the glass, breathe gently in through your nose and keep your mouth open a little.

Firstly, what you want to establish is how intense is the fragrance. Light and delicate or strong and distinctive. Or perhaps somewhere between the two.

Secondly, of the fragrances, are there distinctive aromas of citrus or berries, perhaps flowers, earth and or spice? Does the nose (i.e. smell) suggest sweetness or drying wood? This first sniff is known as identification of the "top notes".

Taste

Take a sip, rest it on your tongue and then swirl it around your mouth. Let the alcohol lift off and wait until the feeling of smooth warmness is on the tongue. You will now be able to taste things like juniper, coriander, citrus, liquorice, or as in some Gins such as Hendrick's, cucumber.

If a greater proportion of botanicals are from roots such as Orris and Angelica, the Gin will taste dryer at the back of your tongue. If it tastes sour the greater proportion will be citrus based.

Does the taste linger? The more intense gins will reveal a lot more botanicals as you take further sips.

Mix

For the purpose of establishing a **GPS** reference for the Gin, just add a single measure of light tonic to a single measure of the gin.

This enables you to identify clearly the intensity and the dryness or sweetness of the gin.

Armed with this basic skill you can now move on to map reading the world of Gin!

Now you need to know what different styles of Gin are there to be tasted…..

Gin styles and reading the Gin map

There are four major style groups

1)   Juniper/citrus style (Classic "London dry")

2)   Spicy/ savoury style

3)   Fruity/ exotic style

4)   Floral/ delicate style

Each has a spot on the 'Gin road map' with the grey areas linking the four styles together, and representing a mixture or blend between the bordering styles.

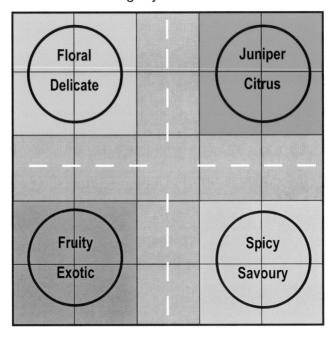

These four key styles are the landmarks used in finding your way around the multitude of gins available, as each have their own characteristics.

By asking only two questions about a gin you can narrow any particular gin to one of the four main "landmarks" on the map.

1) Does the Gin have a strong juniper taste?

Gins that appear in the top half of the map will have the juniper taste clearly coming to the fore when sampled. This is often referred to as the juniper flavour being in the driving seat with other flavours sitting alongside or in the back seat.

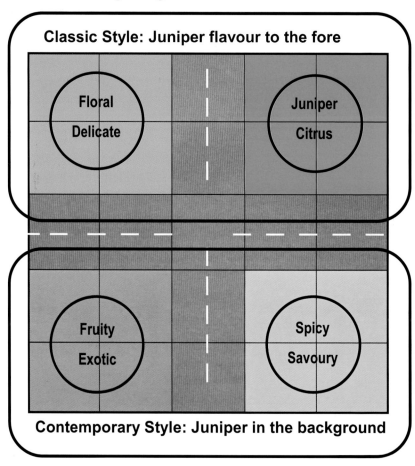

Gins found in the bottom half of the map have something other than the juniper taste to the fore, e.g. Pinkster gin clearly has raspberries as the main flavour. This is often referred to as the raspberry being in the driver's seat and the juniper flavour being in the back seat.

2) Is the Gin lighter or fuller in intensity?

Floral/delicate and fruity/exotic styles tend to be lighter in flavour, whereas juniper/citrus and spicy/savoury tend to be more intense in flavour.

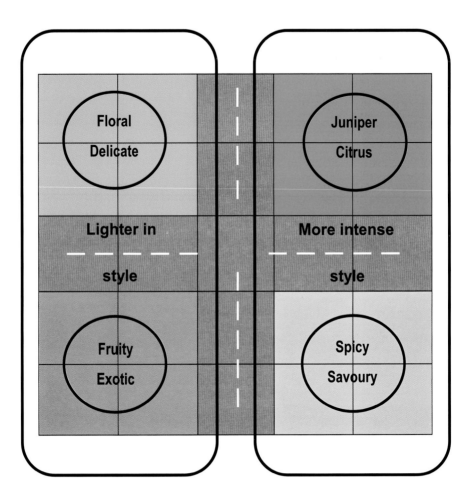

These two steps alone will narrow you down to one of the key styles on the Map.
This is often more than enough detail for the purposes of gin trialling.

Having pinned down the gin to which corner of the map it is positioned in, you now only have to consider if this Gin is:

A) Has a simple distinctive, obvious taste in terms of its flavour, e.g. this is raspberry, rhubarb, peppery or juniper.

Or:

B) Has a complex variety of flavours, with no one flavour being more prominent to another, but so well integrated that it is difficult to identify exactly what may be in the mix.

If the answer is A

Then it will be in one of the four "landmark" coloured areas. With this answer, all you have to do is decide if it is dryer or fruitier/richer than others you have tried.

If the answer is B

Then it will be in one of the grey 'Cross Road' areas.

Beverage Analysis Reference (B.A.R.) System

The Beverage Analysis Reference (B.A.R.) system allows each 'Landmark' and 'Cross Roads' section to be further defined.

This is achieved by dividing the map into 25 squares and then allocating:

(i) a letter for the degree of intenseness (i.e. light through to full/intense as A B C D E respectively) and

(ii) a number for allocating the degree of dryness (i.e. dry though to rich/fruity as 1 2 3 4 5 respectively)

This enables each square to have its own unique reference point .

In the case of Gin, this is the **G**in **P**reference **S**tyle (**GPS**) reference point.

The Gin Preference Style (GPS) References

Gin Style	Light A	B	Medium C	D	Full E
Dry 1	A1	B2	C1	D1	E1
2	A2	B2	C2	D2	E2
Medium 3	A3	B3	C3	D3	E3
4	A4	B4	C4	D4	E4
Rich/Fruity 5	A5	B5	C5	D5	E5

By adding some well known brands to the Map we can start to build up a picture of the styles that you may have tried and enjoyed already.

The logic is quite simple. If you like Bombay Sapphire then it can be said your preference is more than likely a B2 type of gin or something close to it such as a B1 or an A1 or A2 .

We will now look at each of the four keys styles in detail.

Gin Map	Light A	B	Medium C	D	Intense E
Drying 1		Floral			Juniper
2		Delicate			Citrus
		Bombay		Gordons	
Complexity 3					
4		Hendricks		Opihr	Spicy
Richness 5		Fruity Exotic			Savoury

B2

D2

If you are new to the gin world, start your journey with these four. They are widely available in shops and bars across the country.

B4

D4

Chapter 3

Making sense of Gin styles

a) Juniper/Citrus style

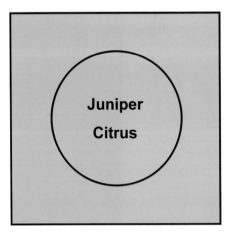

GIN	A	B	C	D	E
1			▓	▓	
2			▓	▓	
3	▓	▓	▓	▓	▓
4			▓		
5			▓		

This section will house the 'Classic' Gin and Tonic styles that have been known for years, a sharp bitter-sweet taste with a citrus edge and a clean finish (i.e. doesn't linger on the taste buds).

Most 'London Dry' Gins fit into this section. 'London dry' refers to the gin making process (a single distillation of botanicals soaked in neutral spirit such as vodka), rather than what a Gin tastes like, or where it was made.

Dilution with water to give the desired alcohol strength is the only 'additive' allowed for the 'London Dry' style of Gin for it to maintain it's quality status. The moment you try to do anything else to the Gin, it loses that 'London Dry' status.

A Classic Gin and Tonic with ice and a slice of lemon is a refreshing drink. The drying effect (from the juniper) and simultaneous tanginess from the coriander (the second most common botanical in gin) excites the taste buds into a mouth-watering zing, leaving you feeling relaxed (by the alcohol!).

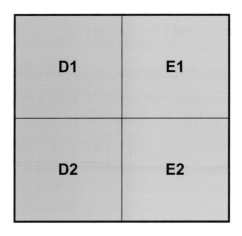

| D1 | E1 |
| D2 | E2 |

Gordon's and Schweppes G & T Ready Mix is one of the bestselling brands of ready mix drinks. By trying one of these you can get an idea of what a Gin from position D2 will taste and feel like.

The Gins on Row 1 will tend to be much drier on the palate than Row 2; and when considering the Columns, column E will be much more intense in flavour than column D. Examples of gin in the specific GPS references are:

D1: 6 'O'Clock Gin
D2: Tarquins
E1: Tanqueray
E2: Bulldog

D1   D2   E1   E2

b) Spicy/Savoury style

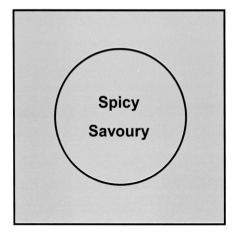

GIN	A	B	C	D	E
1			■		
2			■		
3	■	■	■	■	■
4			■	░	
5			■	░	░

The Gins in this section of the map indicate flavours that would be readily identified when used in cooking, such as herb and spicy based botanicals like thyme, rosemary, olives or pepper.

The Juniper that is used in the process is detectable but only as a secondary, background, complimentary flavour.

It is worth noting here, that occasionally things aren't always what they seem. A pink coloured Gin will tend to reflect the flavour of the fruit used e.g. Pinkster, the raspberry gin that is pink in colour. These are not true "Pink Gins".

Only bottles labeled as 'Pink Gin' or 'Original Pink Gin' are actually Gin with angostura bitters added - so recreating the Pink Gin cocktail. These labeled 'Pink Gins' are truly representative of this savoury section.

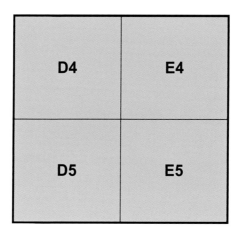

| D4 | E4 |
| D5 | E5 |

Row 5 Gins tend to demonstrate a richness and depth of flavour that signifies a clear example of what the taste of that botanical should be. Row 4 is the same as row 5 but a softer expression of the nature of the botanical.

The intensity of the flavour of Gins from Column E will tend to be longer lasting on the palate than those from column D.

Examples of Gins from these **GPS** references are:

D4: Stratford gin
D5: Opihr oriental gin
E4: Elephant gin
E5: Gin Mare gin

D4   **D5**   **E4**   **E5**

c) Fruity/Exotic style

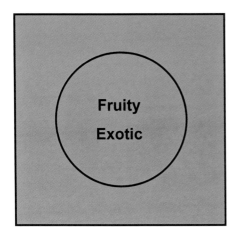

GIN	A	B	C	D	E
1			■		
2			■		
3	■	■	■	■	
4	■		■		
5	■	■	■		

Circle labelled: **Fruity** / **Exotic**

The Gins in this section will clearly have a fruit or exotic flavour as the dominant taste you first encounter on sampling. It can be said that these flavoured Gins remind you of what might be used in the favourite family puddings or jam, such as raspberry, rhubarb and ginger, quince or wild berry.

The majority of people who are asked to try a selection of different Gin and tonics for the first time tend to enjoy this section the most.

These Gins offer clear flavour profiles that the un-initiated can readily identify with. When presented with the right tonics and garnishes, they are in fact encountering 'quality cocktails' which is what makes them so readily acceptable.

It is this section that has exploded in the Gin market, no longer hampered by the traditional expectation of the 'Classic Gin and tonic', promoting experimentation with all sorts combinations.

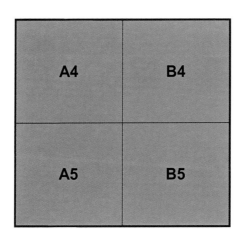

A4	B4
A5	B5

Row 4 flavours tend to be less sweet than row 5 in terms of fruit flavours.

Column B will tend to be more distinctive than column A.

Examples of Gins from these **GPS** references are:

A4:   Voortreker (orange)
A5:   Larios pink (strawberry)
B4:   Pinkster raspberry gin
B5:   Whitley Neil Rhubarb and ginger

| A4 | A5 | B4 | B5 |

d) Floral/Delicate style

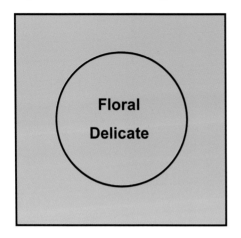

GIN	A	B	C	D	E
1					
2					
3					
4					
5					

It can be said that the Gins in this section often reflect 'garden' botanicals, i.e. those that offer fragrance and colour, such as heathers, rose petals, hibiscus, elderflowers and lavender.

Generally speaking, the objective of Gin making is to extract the pure essences of the different botanicals and get them into the alcohol. This can be done a number of ways as outlined before in Chapter 1.

When the metal tea bag approach to Gin making is used, a much lighter more fragrant style is produced and many of these type of Gins are found in this section.

The botanicals used are still the same as many other London Dry gins, but often Angelica and Orris Root are botanicals that add a perfume element to a Gin. Chamomile, elderflower or geraniums also add extra delicate fragrances to a finish of a Gin.

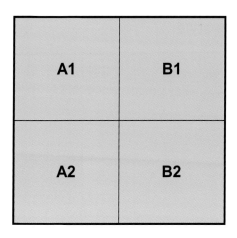

Row 1 Gins tend to be less fragrant than Row 2. Column B will tend to be more distinctive than column A.

Examples of Gins from these **GPS** references are:

A1: Silent Pool
A2: Rock Rose
B1: Bloom
B2: Greenhook Ginsmith

e) The Gin Cross Roads style

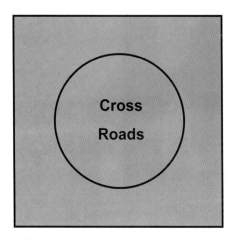

GIN	A	B	C	D	E
1					
2					
3					
4					
5					

The **Cross Roads** that separate the four styles represent all the Gins that are a cross between the styles bordering on to it.

They demonstrate a degree of elegance whereby no single flavour is actually jumping to the fore more than any other, but is the amalgamation of the different botanicals in harmony with each other.

The C1 and C2 are a cross, or half way house, in terms of the taste profile between the floral/delicate and full juniper styles. The A3 and B3 are a blend of the floral and fruity styles.

The D3 and E3 are a blend of the full juniper and the savoury/spicy styles and the C4 and C5 are a cross between the fruity and spicy/savoury styles.

C3 represents the really complex gins that have some of all the four key areas in it's 'blend'.

These **Cross Road** references on the grid will house some of the finest gins available.

Examples of Gins from the cross road **GPS**'s are:

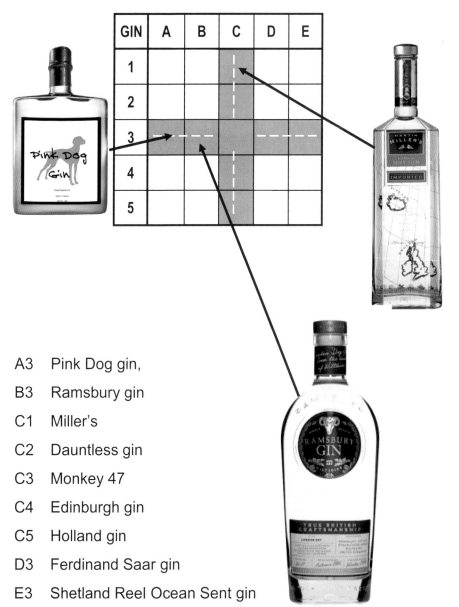

GIN	A	B	C	D	E
1					
2					
3					
4					
5					

A3   Pink Dog gin,

B3   Ramsbury gin

C1   Miller's

C2   Dauntless gin

C3   Monkey 47

C4   Edinburgh gin

C5   Holland gin

D3   Ferdinand Saar gin

E3   Shetland Reel Ocean Sent gin

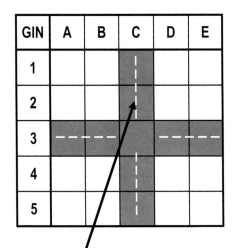

GIN	A	B	C	D	E
1					
2					
3					
4					
5					

C2

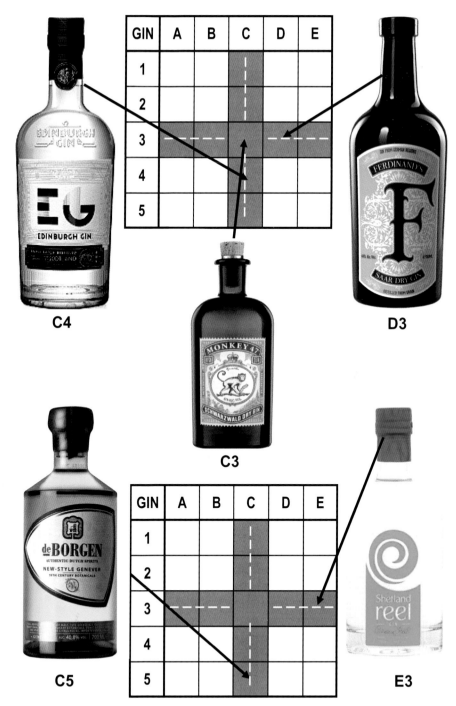

C4

GIN	A	B	C	D	E
1					
2					
3					
4					
5					

D3

C3

C5

GIN	A	B	C	D	E
1					
2					
3					
4					
5					

E3

Other Gin Styles

There are two other styles of Gin available, the 'Old Tom' style Gins, and the 'Navy Strength' Gins.

'Old Tom' gins are sweetened gins. This style became popular in the18th century with the rough alcohol being sweetened to make it drinkable.

The quality of the Gin is not in question, but the sweetened style has come back into fashion to enable bartenders recreate the classic 'Tom Collins' cocktail.

Since they are only used for cocktails, they shouldn't really be classified in the standard Gin Sat Nav grid, as they would appear on a 6th Row.

Gin Style	Light A	B	Medium C	D	Full E
Dry 1					
2					
Medium 3					
4					
Rich/Fruity 5					
Old Tom 6					

'Navy Strength' gins are gins where the alcohol level is 57.5% proof or higher. As the name suggests, the Royal Navy had Gin produced at this strength.

Proof is exactly what it implies; gunpowder would be mixed with the gin and if it ignited when lit, it proved that the gin had not been diluted!

As with the "Old Tom" gins, they don't fit the standard Gin Sat Nav grid - they would appear as a column F (with rows 1-5). By their very nature, they are intense in style and are mainly used in cocktails.

Gin Style	Light A	B	Medium C	D	Full E	Navy F
Dry 1						
2						
Medium 3						
4						
Rich/ Fruity 5						

Chapter 4

Making sense of Tonics

Indian Tonic and a lighter version of Indian Tonic are the tonics that are most commonly known, even though for many years there have been many different types of tonics available in cocktail bars.

With the surge in interest in Gin, tonics have received a new burst of life, bringing real colour and dimension to the 'Gin and Tonic' drink we know today.

Standard or light tonics will work with Gins from all sections of the Gin map. Without a doubt **some of the specialist tonics noticeably enhance the finished taste** of the Gin and Tonic drink.

What is tonic? Why is it so important?

Tonic is simply carbonated water that has quinine added (quinine gives it a bitter taste). It is then blended with other fruit extracts and sweeteners to give it balance and make it an acceptable soft drink.

It is important because, as Fever-Tree rightly point out, it is two-thirds of a Classic Gin and tonic. This is the most common way of enjoying Gin. **So getting the right tonic with the right Gin is a quest worth exploring**.

New cocktail versions are often made live on the spot by the mixologist in cocktail bars. In other words, the tonic is made there and then, along with all the tweaks and garnishes required.

Fever-Tree have standardised a few mixers which have proved to be versatile with all sorts of Gin. Each Gin maker can now take these standard tonics and soon work out a perfect serve for their Gin creation.

The styles of tonic that are readily found are:-

Light, Standard, Mediterranean, Elderflower, Aromatic, and Fruity such as Clementine. An extravagant tonic would be Champagne or Prosecco, at a push!

So the question is, which came first, the resurgence in the popularity of tonics and then Gin; or the other way round? Does it matter? Perhaps not, because there is now a whole range of quality tonics to choose from with over a 1000 Gins to mix them with. Some purists want more bubbles, others want less.

The different tonics offer varying degrees of fizz. If you want gin and tonic bursting forth and splashing up your nose then use Schweppes, as they put far more gas into the tonic than most other brands. Schweppes tonic does add to the enjoyment when added to some of the classic London Dry gins on a hot summer day!

The history of tonic is really the history of quinine, a medicine used to treat the symptoms of malaria.

As people travelled and discovered the Americas in the 1600's they suffered from malaria. They learnt that extracts from the bark of the cinchona tree (local name quina-quina) reduced the fever symptoms of malaria. It was known as the Jesuit's bark and became a very valuable commodity, traded all over the known world.

When King Charles II was cured of malaria using quinine, its acceptance as the main anti-malaria treatment was firmly established. Its use continued until the 1940's when modern drugs took over.

Initially the bark was ground down into a powder, which was very bitter in taste, which was then added to a liquid and drunk.

When the British were in India, the quinine was mixed with sweetened water, thus effectively the 'Indian Tonic Water' was born. Mr Schweppes then developed the carbonation method and the sparkling tonic as we know it today was established.

Tonic Styles and the Gin Map

In general terms, tonic can be put into one of four categories

    a) Lighter tonic
    b) Neutral/Standard tonics
    c) Sweeter/Fruitier tonics
    d) Aromatic tonic

When you consider the range of gins available it's easy to see that the four style groups of Gin need to be approached differently. Just as the Gins can be classified, so can the tonics!

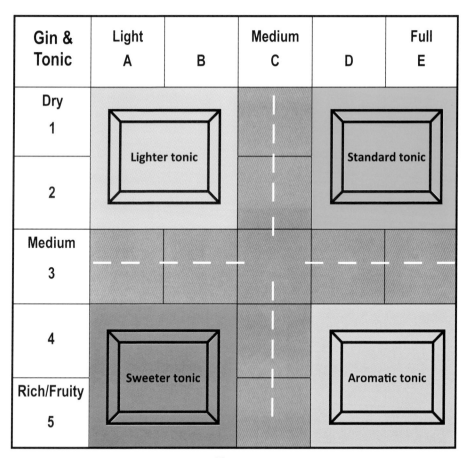

Gin & Tonic	Light A	B	Medium C	D	Full E
Dry 1					
2	Lighter tonic			Standard tonic	
Medium 3					
4					
Rich/Fruity 5	Sweeter tonic			Aromatic tonic	

a) Light Tonics

	A	B	C	D	E
1					
2					
3					
4					
5					

Distillers Choice Dry Indian Tonic Water

This is one of the lowest sugar, all natural tonic waters. This tonic specifically has the minimum carbonation to allow the flavour and unique character of the Gin to express itself.

Fever-Tree Naturally Light Tonic

This has some 50% less sugars than its full Indian brother. This is a nice crisp tonic water bringing quinine, citrus and aromatic botanicals together with natural fruit sugars and soft spring water.

b) Sweeter Tonics

	A	B	C	D	E
1			▓		
2			▓		
3	▓	▓	▓	▓	▓
4	▓	▓	▓		
5	▓	▓	▓		

Merchant Heart Hibiscus Tonic

Hibiscus tonic gives a rich fruity tone with a sweetish finish.

Elderflower Tonic

This delicate flavour of elderflower is balanced with the soft bitterness of the quinine. Its slight sweetness lends itself to the more fruity gins or to make a less dry 'London Dry' Gin and tonic.

c) Aromatic Tonics

GIN	A	B	C	D	E
1			▓		
2			▓		
3	▓		▓	▓	▓
4			▓	░	
5			▓	░	

Fentimans 19:05 Herbal Tonic

A delicate herbal tonic has a bitter-sweet effect from the quinine and lime blossoms rounded off by a hint of juniper.

Fever-Tree Mediterranean Tonic

Flowers, fruits and herbs are gathered from around the Mediterranean shores, their oils are blended with high quality quinine from the fever trees of Congo creating this unique and delicate floral tonic.

d) Standard Tonic

GIN	A	B	C	D	E
1					
2					
3					
4					
5					

Fever-Tree Indian Tonic

This is a soft tonic with a sparkle like that of champagne. It has a refreshing hint of citrus balanced by the bitterness of the natural quinine, giving a crisp clean finish. Great with 'London Dry' Gins.

Thomas Henry Tonic Water

This tonic water is refreshingly full of flavour, even though it has a noticeably high quinine content, giving it an initial distinctive bitter taste. It balances out most Gins in the juniper/citrus style beautifully, being a favourite in many cocktail bars over the years.

e) Cross Road Tonics

GIN	A	B	C	D	E
1					
2					
3					
4					
5					

Gins in the grey (cross road) section work well with light tonics.

As these Gins are like a halfway house between two styles, more than several styles of tonic can work well to enhance the finished taste.

Another way to work out the ideal Gin and tonic combination for this cross road section, is to use the phone app called **GINVENTORY**. This app lists many of these Gins and shows what the 'peoples choice' preferences for tonics and garnishes are for a particular Gin.

The Gin-Tonic Scales

Having discovered which Gin may go with which tonic; the next thing is to work out how much tonic to put with the Gin.

A good approach is to start tasting the Gin - have just a sip to get a feel of the neat spirit.

1) Then add a cube of ice and sip it again.

2) Then add the same measure of tonic as you have of the Gin. This is called a 1:1 ratio. This starts to open up the Gin's characteristics.

3) Then add a second measure of tonic. This is called the 2:1 ratio. This dilutes the effect of the alcohol and enables the flavours in the Gin to come to the fore on the palate.

4) Then add a third measure of tonic. This is called the 3:1 ratio. Most Gin and tonic drinks are at their best with a 3:1 ratio.

5) On a warm day when you want a longer drink, 4:1 ratio is often the best.

Some Gins need only a 1:1 ratio, while others need the 3:1 ratio to get the best taste. Gins found in the fruity section often can take the 3 to 4:1 ratio because the flavours are so distinct and are not affected by the volume of the tonic. Some of the complex delicate Gins just need a splash of tonic to let the flavours express themselves.

If you adopt this step-by-step approach you can soon establish the ratio that suits you best for any particular Gin.

Chapter 5

Making sense of Garnishes

Adding garnish to a Gin and tonic is like adding accessories and perfume for a perfect outfit.

Adding a garnish to a Gin releases a sense of freshness to enhance the sensory experience. The garnish can be either complimentary (mint and raspberry) or contrasting (rosemary and mango).

Top Tip

Some garnishes can be frozen into an ice cube, such as a raspberry and a leaf of mint.

This means you are ready at any time to enjoy your favourite Gin and tonic.

The Gin Map has four key areas that show dominant flavour profiles. Just as with the tonics, there are key types of garnishes that will suit each of the four main styles.

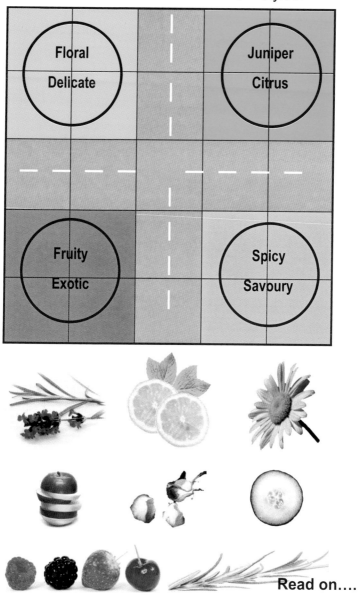

Floral		Juniper
Delicate		Citrus
Fruity		Spicy
Exotic		Savoury

Read on....

a) Juniper and Citrus garnishes

These naturally lean towards any citrus fruit, such as lime, lemon, orange or even grapefruit. Since most Gins in this section are 'London Dry' the very nature of how it is made means that there are no natural sweeteners or flavours added to the gin.

The use of these type of fruits add an element of colour and drama to the Gin and tonic along with a perceived hint of sweetness.

GIN	A	B	C	D	E
1					
2					
3					
4					
5					

Some Gins recommend using pink grapefruit to garnish their Gin.

b) Floral and Delicate garnishes

The Gins in this section require garnishes that will not overpower the delicate aromas and flavours. Cucumber or a slice of apple will just add a softness in the background.

Less intrusive are rose petals or flowers that will add an extra hint of fragrance. Lavender can offer an extra lift with Gins that had lavender used in their distilling.

A little citrus peel adds more fragrance than flavour.

Hibiscus flowers has a sour taste yet when added to the Gin enhances and gives added fragrance.

GIN	A	B	C	D	E
1					
2					
3					
4					
5					

c) Fruity and Exotic garnishes

The individual Gins in this section clearly have distinctive flavour profiles such as raspberries, orange and rhubarb and ginger.

The best garnish is either the peel of the fruit in question or the fruit itself e.g. for **Pinkster Gin**, a fresh raspberry works perfectly, but what adds finesse is when you put a leaf of mint in with it.

GIN	A	B	C	D	E
1					
2					
3					
4					
5					

The aim is to either **amplify or contrast** the Gin flavour or do both as in the Pinkster Gin example.

d) Savoury and Spicy garnishes

These work with all things savoury, e.g. rosemary, olive, thyme, rocket or orange, cloves, chilli or pepper.

Gin Mare is a Gin that has been distilled using olives, thyme, basil and rosemary. It is a very distinctive flavoured Gin. When you add Mediterranean tonic (3:1) and ice and **just one leaf** of rosemary dropped into the Gin, it gives it a real Mediterranean feel. Then, if you add just a small piece of mango, you will feel like you have been transported to the Bahamas.

If you feel like going to heaven, you then add one crack of black pepper!

This is a great example of what a difference the garnish makes.

GIN	A	B	C	D	E
1					
2					
3					
4					
5					

e) Cross Road Garnishes

Garnishes for the "Cross Road" Gins are often determined by the botanicals in the Gin, either complimenting or contrasting the main botanicals used.

As with the tonics, they can overlap with one of the four key styles.

GIN	A	B	C	D	E
1					
2					
3					
4					
5					

Any one of these seven garnishes work with this (C3) Gin

Sage

Lime

Pink Pepper   **Orange Peel**

Orange   **Blackberry**   **Cranberry**

The Gin Preference Style (GPS)

So there you have it - The solution to the Gin, Tonic and Garnish jigsaw - a system for categorising Gin that describes the relationship between one Gin and another, how best to complement them with tonics and garnishes, that enables you to define your own personal preference.

So what is your GPS?

Gin Style	Light A	B	Medium C	D	Full E
Dry 1	A1	B2	C1	D1	E1
2	A2	B2	C2	D2	E2
Medium 3	A3	B3	C3	D3	E3
4	A4	B4	C4	D4	E4
Rich/Fruity 5	A5	B5	C5	D5	E5

ImaGINe yourself now cruising the world of Gin

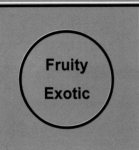

Fruity

Exotic

Your
Notes

A4	B4
A5	B5

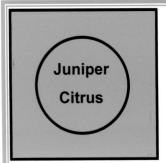

Your
Notes

D1	E1
D2	E2

Floral

Delicate

Your

Notes

A1	B1
A2	B2

Spicy
Savoury

Your
Notes

D4	E4
D5	E5

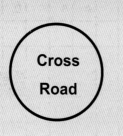

Cross
Road

Your
Notes

	A	B	C	D	E
1			■		
2			■		
3					
4					
5					

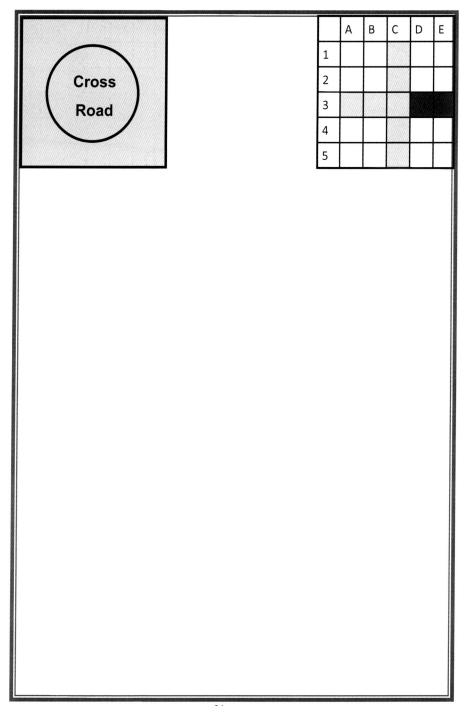

	A	B	C	D	E
1					
2					
3					
4					
5					

Cross Road

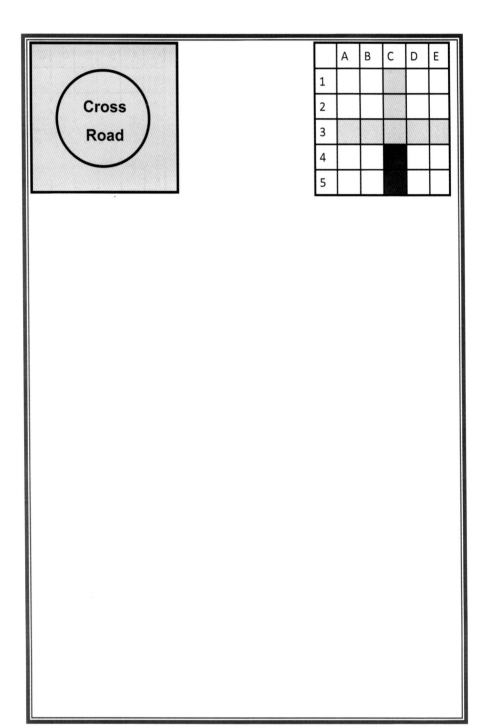

Cross
Road

	A	B	C	D	E
1					
2					
3					
4					
5					

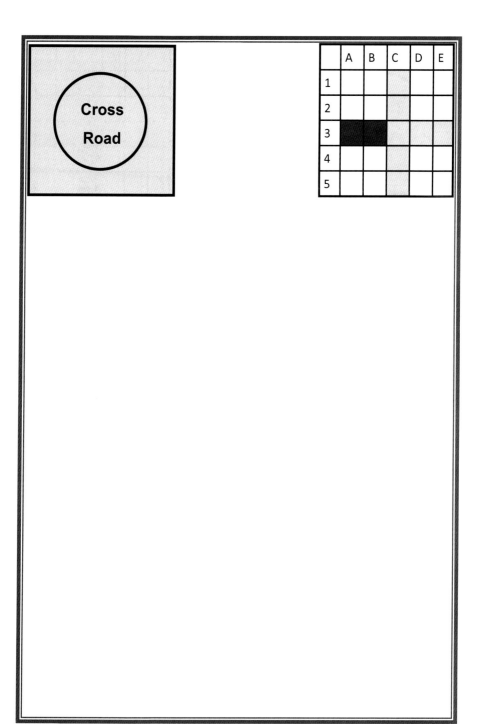

	A	B	C	D	E
1					
2					
3					
4					
5					

Cross Road

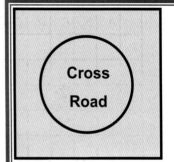

	A	B	C	D	E
1					
2					
3					
4					
5					

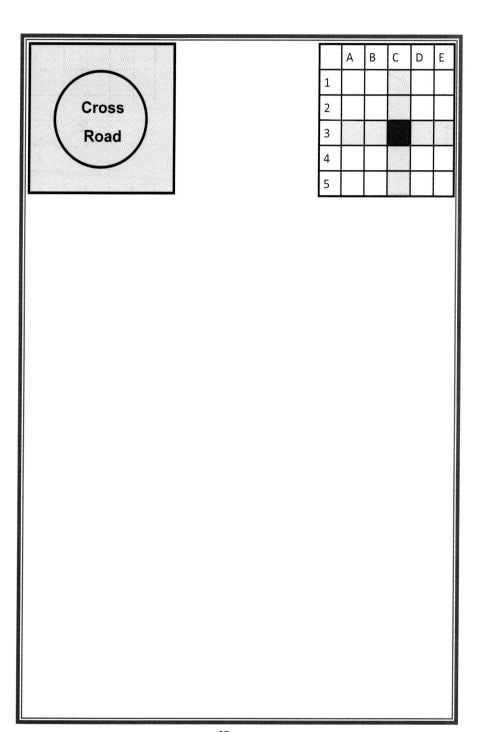

	A	B	C	D	E
1					
2					
3			■		
4					
5					

The Gin Sat Nav

By David Hitchens

This publication is part of a series of Tipple Rated products and publications. For more information, please visit:

http://www.thenewwineshop.co.uk

Also: **yourtipple.com**

Copyright 2017 David Hitchens.

ALL RIGHTS RESERVED.